Epic Disasters

THE WORST HURRICANES OF ALL TIME

by Terri Dougherty

Consultant:
Susan L. Cutter, PhD
Director
Hazards and Vulnerability Research Institute
University of South Carolina

CAPSTONE PRESS
a capstone imprint

Edge Books are published by Capstone Press,
1710 Roe Crest Drive, North Mankato, Minnesota 56003.
www.capstonepub.com

Library of Congress Cataloging-in-Publication Data
Dougherty, Terri.
  The worst hurricanes of all time / by Terri Dougherty.
    p. cm.—(Edge books. epic disasters)
  Includes bibliographical references and index.
  Summary: "Describes the worst hurricanes in history, as well as formation, scale,
and disaster tips"—Provided by publisher.
  ISBN 978-1-4296-7659-5 (library binding)
  ISBN 978-1-4296-8014-1 (paperback)
  1. Hurricanes—History. I. Title. II. Series.
  QC944.2D727 2012
  363.34'922—dc23   2011037598

Editorial Credits
Anthony Wacholtz, editor; Veronica Correia, designer; Marcie Spence,
    media researcher; Laura Manthe, production specialist

Photo Credits
Alamy: RGB Ventures/SuperStock, 29; Getty Images: Bettmann, 13, 14, 21,
22, 25, 27, Library of Congress, 9, Paul J. Richards/AFP, 6, Robert Galbraith/
AFP, 18; Mary Evans Picture Library: 11; Shutterstock: B747, 5, romarti
(design element), Sascha Burkard, cover (tree), 19, 28, Vladislav Gurfinkel,
cover (hurricane)

TABLE OF CONTENTS

A HURRICANE'S AWESOME POWER

Towering waves pound the shore. Driving winds uproot trees and batter buildings. Rain slaps the earth. An incredibly powerful hurricane has arrived.

Hurricanes are huge spinning storm systems. They begin as a group of thunderstorms over an ocean and gain strength from the warm water. Warm, moist air feeds the storms. Light winds help the storms grow. If conditions are right, the storms begin to spin and become one massive storm.

Once winds reach 74 miles (119 kilometers) per hour, the spinning storm is a hurricane. A hurricane can last days or several weeks. The storm is considered a hurricane until the winds drop below 74 mph.

The strongest hurricanes have winds of more than 150 miles (240 km) per hour. Their awesome power can destroy buildings and tear beaches apart. These storms can easily toss the roofs off of buildings and put trees on their sides. Hurricanes often cause flooding. They sometimes cause tornadoes to form.

RANKING HURRICANES

Hurricanes are ranked on a scale of 1 to 5. A category 5 hurricane is the most powerful.

CATEGORY 1 Winds of 74 to 95 mph (119 to 153 kph)

CATEGORY 2 Winds of 96 to 110 mph (154 to 177 kph)

CATEGORY 3 Winds of 111 to 130 mph (179 to 209 kph)

CATEGORY 4 Winds of 131 to 155 mph (211 to 249 kph)

CATEGORY 5 Winds of more than 155 mph (249 kph)

FACT:
Hurricanes go by many names. The common name for these natural disasters is tropical cyclone. If they happen in the north Atlantic Ocean, Gulf of Mexico, or Caribbean Sea, they are called hurricanes. They are called typhoons if they occur in the northwest Pacific Ocean west of the international date line.

A COSTLY DISASTER

DATE: August 16-28, 1992

LOCATION: southwestern Florida, northwestern Bahamas, southwestern Louisiana

TOP RATING: Category 5

FACT:
The wind from Hurricane Andrew blew the radar off the roof of the National Hurricane Center.

radar—a weather tool that sends out waves to determine the size, strength, and movement of storms

Hurricane Andrew is known for destruction. When the hurricane hit, boats rammed the shore. Groves of trees toppled. Trucks tipped over, and homes became piles of rubble.

Small but intense, Andrew was one of the costliest hurricanes of all time. Entire neighborhoods were crushed when it struck southern Florida on August 24, 1992. Almost every mobile home in the city of Homestead was destroyed. The buildings at a local U.S. Air Force base were crumpled.

The hurricane also hit the northwestern Bahamas and southwestern Louisiana. But most of the damage was done in Florida. By the time it was over, Andrew's damage added up to $26.5 billion in the United States alone.

ANDREW'S PATH

The Bahamas were the first to feel Andrew's strength. It hit on August 23 with winds of at least 131 miles (211 km) per hour. It grew even stronger as it moved to Florida. It struck Florida on August 24 with winds possibly reaching 165 miles (266 km) per hour. From there, it crossed the Gulf of Mexico and hit Louisiana on August 26. Although the wind speed had dropped, the storm still tore roofs off of homes.

UNEXPECTED HURRICANE

DATE: August 27-September 8, 1900
LOCATION: Galveston, Texas
TOP RATING: Category 4

In 1900 few people thought Galveston, Texas, was in danger of being hit by a hurricane. The booming port city was on an island off the Texas coast, an area not known for hurricanes. But at the end of August, a storm began to grow in the Atlantic Ocean.

Weather forecasters said the storm would turn north. But forecaster Isaac Cline was not so sure. He was in Galveston and noticed that the water was rising. He warned people to get to higher ground.

The hurricane hit in the early evening on September 8. Pounding waves and winds of more than 130 miles (209 km) per hour tore at wooden buildings. A **storm surge** of at least 15.5 feet (4.7 meters) covered the entire island. It crushed buildings and pushed forward a huge wall of **debris**.

storm surge—a huge wave of water pushed ashore by an approaching hurricane
debris—the scattered pieces of something that has been broken or destroyed

After his home broke apart, Cline made it through the storm by clinging to a piece of debris. Many others weren't so lucky. Between 6,000 and 12,000 people died in the nation's most deadly natural disaster. For much of his life, Cline worked to improve storm predictions so no other city would suffer as Galveston had.

THE GREAT HURRICANE OF 1780

DATE: October 9–20, 1780
LOCATION: Caribbean Sea
TOP RATING: likely Category 4

One hurricane is known not only for its incredible destruction, but also how it affected a war. It may have helped the Americans win the Revolutionary War.

In 1780 the Americans were fighting for independence from Great Britain. Many British ships were sailing in the Caribbean Sea. The crews were surprised by the Great Hurricane of 1780 on October 10. The British fleet near St. Lucia was battered and destroyed by the storm for more than a week. Near Bermuda, more British ships sank.

The lost ships weakened the British navy. This may have helped the Americans win the war.

MONSTER STORM

British sailors were not the only ones to feel the storm's fury. The hurricane swirled from Barbados to Bermuda with deadly force. It wiped out villages on the islands of Barbados, Martinique, Puerto Rico, and St. Lucia.

A CYCLONE OF CHANGE

DATE: November 7-13, 1970
LOCATION: East Pakistan (present-day Bangladesh)
TOP RATING: Category 3

The land where the Ganges River meets the Bay of Bengal is prone to flooding. The coast is always at risk when strong storms move through. On November 13, 1970, it was the site of the worst hurricane disaster in history.

Even before hitting land, the storm proved its power. In the Bay of Bengal, its winds reached 115 miles (185 km) per hour. Driving rain sank a huge ship weighing more than 5,000 tons (4,536 metric tons).

A towering surge of water hit the shore of Bhola in present-day Bangladesh. The 20-foot (6.1-m) wall of water swept up buildings, trees, and animals. Three-quarters of the homes in the area were destroyed. Some experts believe the storm killed 500,000 people. The survivors were left with little food or water. The storm had killed much of their livestock.

STORM BRINGS CHANGE

The people who survived the Bhola cyclone needed help getting food and water. They suffered from widespread famine and disease. After their government offered little aid, citizens fought to be independent. They succeeded in 1971. Before the storm, the area was called East Pakistan. After the storm and the citizens' independence, it became the country of Bangladesh.

LABOR DAY HURRICANE OF 1935

DATE: August 29-September 10, 1935

LOCATION: Florida Keys

TOP RATING: Category 5

Writer Ernest Hemingway was shocked at the sight of the bare island. Not even a blade of grass was standing. The ground was covered with eels, crawfish, and shells that should have been on the bottom of the sea.

The hurricane that swept across the Florida Keys on September 2, 1935, hurled a huge surge of water over the islands. The waves and wind were strong enough to push over a train. The wall of water washed away railroad tracks built 30 feet (9.1 m) above sea level. A ship was blown more than 3 miles (4.8 km) **inland**.

The hurricane's winds of 150 to 200 miles (241 to 322 km) per hour ripped away trees, homes, and bridges. A building's 18-foot (5.5-m) beam was tossed 900 feet (274 m) into another building. The glass at the top of a lighthouse was broken.

People struggled to survive the storm. One man who was blown into the water grabbed on to a tree. He was knocked out during the storm. When he awoke, he found himself in a tree 20 feet (6.1 m) above the ground. Another survivor said, "I put my flashlight out on sea and could see walls of water."

FACT:
The stronger a storm is, the lower its air pressure is. The Labor Day Hurricane had the lowest air pressure at landfall of any hurricane hitting the United States.

inland—away from the ocean
landfall—the area where a hurricane moves over land

HURRICANE KATRINA

DATE: August 23-30, 2005
LOCATION: southeastern United States, Bahamas, Cuba
TOP RATING: Category 5

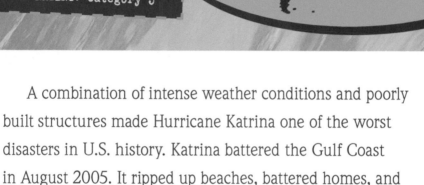

A combination of intense weather conditions and poorly built structures made Hurricane Katrina one of the worst disasters in U.S. history. Katrina battered the Gulf Coast in August 2005. It ripped up beaches, battered homes, and knocked down forests.

Katrina struck Florida first. It moved across Florida's southern tip with winds of more than 75 miles (121 km) per hour. At least 15 inches (38 centimeters) of rain resulted in widespread floods in the area.

The hurricane grew stronger over the Gulf of Mexico. At one point, its winds reached 170 miles (274 km) per hour, making it a Category 5 hurricane.

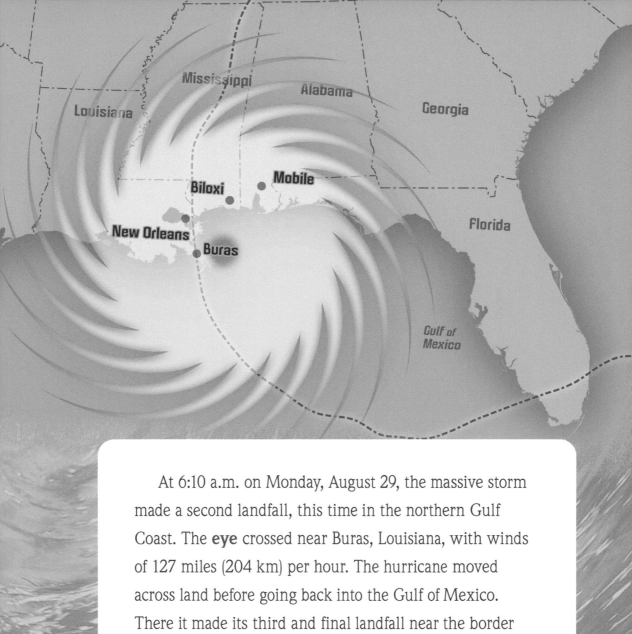

At 6:10 a.m. on Monday, August 29, the massive storm
made a second landfall, this time in the northern Gulf
Coast. The **eye** crossed near Buras, Louisiana, with winds
of 127 miles (204 km) per hour. The hurricane moved
across land before going back into the Gulf of Mexico.
There it made its third and final landfall near the border
of Mississippi and Louisiana. In nearby New Orleans, the
wind blew out windows in hotels and office buildings.
In Biloxi, Mississippi, waves and winds crushed homes.
Power lines toppled and walls shook in Mobile, Alabama.

eye—central, calm area at the center of a hurricane

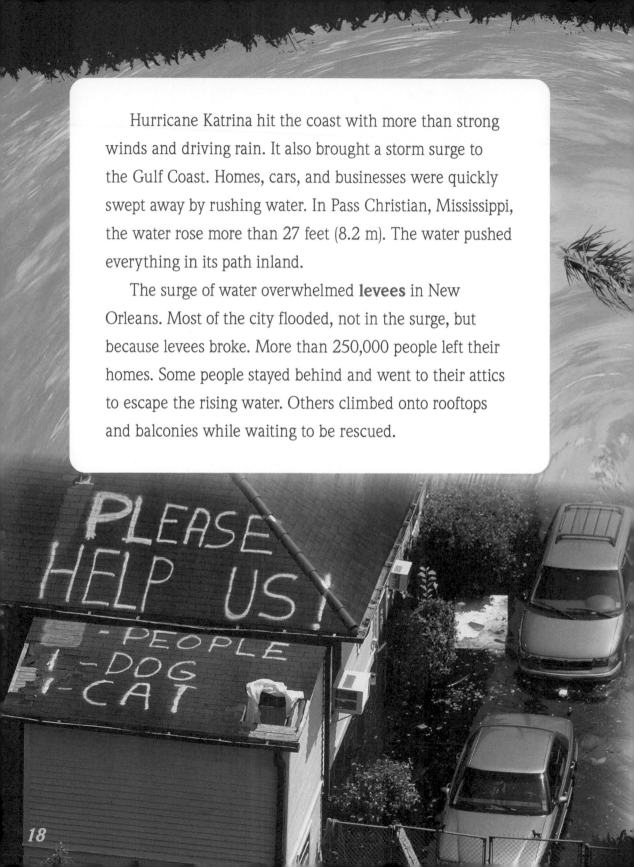

Hurricane Katrina hit the coast with more than strong winds and driving rain. It also brought a storm surge to the Gulf Coast. Homes, cars, and businesses were quickly swept away by rushing water. In Pass Christian, Mississippi, the water rose more than 27 feet (8.2 m). The water pushed everything in its path inland.

The surge of water overwhelmed **levees** in New Orleans. Most of the city flooded, not in the surge, but because levees broke. More than 250,000 people left their homes. Some people stayed behind and went to their attics to escape the rising water. Others climbed onto rooftops and balconies while waiting to be rescued.

Katrina left many people without power, water, or homes. The storm claimed more than 1,800 lives.

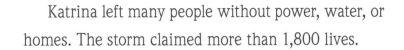

TIMELINE

AUGUST 23: Katrina begins as a storm in the Bahamas.

AUGUST 25: Katrina hits Florida at 5:30 p.m. as a Category 1 hurricane.

AUGUST 28: Katrina strengthens to a Category 5 hurricane in the Gulf of Mexico.

AUGUST 29: Katrina hits the Louisiana coast around 6:00 a.m. as a Category 3 hurricane. The storm surge pushes water over the top of some levees. After the storm passes, breaks appear in the levees in New Orleans. The Mississippi coast has severe flooding caused by a storm surge.

AUGUST 30: Levee failures cause more than 80 percent of New Orleans to flood.

levee—a structure or raised area built to hold back water and prevent flooding

HURRICANE CAMILLE

DATE: August 14–22, 1969
LOCATION: southeastern
United States, Cuba
TOP RATING: Category 5

With winds estimated at 200 miles (322 km) per hour, Camille was one of the worst hurricanes to hit the Gulf Coast. It struck around midnight on August 17, 1969. The storm brought wind, storm surges, and rain that caused about $1.4 billion in damage.

Camille reached land east of Bay St. Louis, Mississippi. A new railroad bridge over the bay was destroyed as the storm tossed the heavy rails into the water. The storm surge reached 25 feet (7.6 m) in Pass Christian, Mississippi. A few miles away in Buras, Louisiana, almost every home was destroyed. When it moved inland, Camille was not done causing destruction. It brought up to 31 inches (79 cm) of rain and flash floods to Virginia and West Virginia.

One person described the invading water. "When the tide started to rise fast, it all seemed to come at once. Before you knew it, the water was knee deep. And a few minutes later it was up to the waist."

After the storm, people tried to return to their homes in Venice, Louisiana. Many found they had no homes to return to. Houses had been broken apart and blown into the marsh.

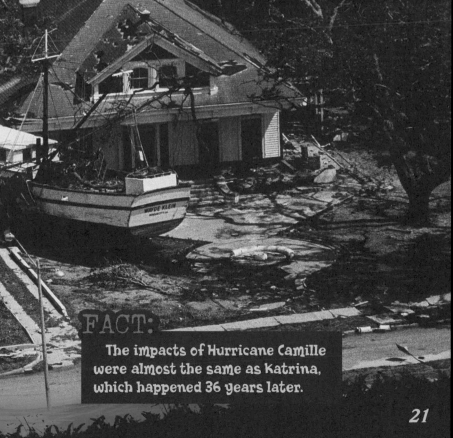

FACT:

The impacts of Hurricane Camille were almost the same as Katrina, which happened 36 years later.

WASHED AWAY

DATE: October 22–November 5, 1998
LOCATION: Central America
TOP RATING: Category 5

Hurricane Mitch was one of the most devastating hurricanes ever recorded. Mitch made landfall on October 29, 1998, in Honduras. As it moved over the mountains of Central America, it brought an enormous amount of rainfall. Some areas in Honduras and Nicaragua received more than 6 feet (1.8 m) of rain.

All the rain couldn't gather on the mountain or soak into the soil. It ran down the mountainside, causing **mudslides** and flooding that wiped out entire villages. Roads and bridges were washed away.

The damage caused by Mitch was severe. Millions were left homeless. Banana and corn crops were destroyed. Fresh water became scarce. The hurricane killed more than 11,000 people, making it the deadliest hurricane in the Atlantic Ocean in 200 years.

SUPER-TYPHOON NINA

Super-typhoon Nina also caused extreme flooding. The storm moved over China in 1975 and stalled, bringing record rainfall. There was so much water that a dam collapsed. The disaster killed more than 200,000 people and cost the area $1.2 billion.

mudslide—a flow of rock, earth, and debris mixed with water
stall—to come to a stop

THE LONG ISLAND EXPRESS

DATE: September 10-22, 1938
LOCATION: northeastern United States
TOP RATING: Category 3

The morning of September 21, 1938, was pleasant and sunny on Long Island, New York. No one guessed disaster was speeding toward the area.

The sky turned cloudy and some people thought it looked yellow. Then the weather quickly got worse. A hurricane moved into the area so fast that it became known as the Long Island Express.

The hurricane hit Long Island around 2:20 p.m. Cottages on the beach in Connecticut and Rhode Island were washed away. One family survived by holding onto the attic floor when their house broke apart.

The storm shoved boats and debris inland. A train heading into Connecticut had to push away a house as it headed toward the station.

The hurricane's storm surge brought more disasters. The streets of downtown Hartford, Connecticut, flooded. Twenty feet (6.1 m) of water covered parts of Providence, Rhode Island. In New London, Connecticut, power lines fell. The sparks lit a fire that burned much of the city.

HURRICANE IRENE

The East Coast was again hit by a hurricane in 2011. Hurricane Irene hit North Carolina on August 27 as a Category 1 hurricane and moved north. The storm grew stronger and moved inland. It brought flooding to New Jersey, Vermont, and northern New York. The storm caused billions of dollars in damage.

HURRICANE DONNA

DATE: August 29-September 13, 1960
LOCATION: Puerto Rico, Cuba, Bahamas, eastern United States
TOP RATING: Category 5

Hurricane Donna was the storm that wouldn't quit. On September 10, 1960, it hit Florida and barreled up the East Coast. It is the only storm to bring hurricane-force winds to Florida, North Carolina, and New England.

Winds reached 180 miles (290 km) per hour before the storm hit land. Then Donna blasted into the Florida Keys. One person recalled, "We thought the house wasn't going to make it. It shook. It rattled. We thought it was going to come down. It was scary."

Naples and Fort Myers in Florida were next to feel Donna's power. Trees in the Everglades toppled to the ground as the storm roared for 36 hours. Oranges and grapefruit were thrown from trees.

Donna then entered the Atlantic Ocean and turned northeast. Winds of more than 80 miles (129 km) per hour pounded North Carolina. Then the storm moved up the coast. In Rhode Island, winds reached 130 miles (209 km) per hour. A storm surge of up to 9 feet (2.7 m) rolled into the state.

Donna finally lost steam over Canada. The hurricane had traveled more than 2,000 miles (3,219 km).

TIMELINE

AUGUST 29: Donna begins to form off Africa's coast.

SEPTEMBER 1: Winds reach hurricane strength.

SEPTEMBER 2: Donna becomes a Category 4 hurricane.

SEPTEMBER 7: Donna passes through the Bahamas.

SEPTEMBER 10: Donna hits the Florida Keys as a Category 4 and moves up the west coast of Florida. The storm surge reaches 13 feet (4 m).

SEPTEMBER 11: Donna turns right and crosses Florida into the Atlantic Ocean.

SEPTEMBER 12: Donna strikes North Carolina and moves into New England.

SEPTEMBER 13: Donna weakens over Maine and eastern Canada.

LIVING WITH HURRICANES

If there's a chance a hurricane may develop in a region, the National Weather Service (NWS) issues a hurricane watch. A watch means there's a chance a hurricane will hit, so people should prepare for the storm. Put boards across windows. Listen to the radio and TV for hurricane information.

If a hurricane is expected to hit, the NWS will issue a hurricane warning. Leave your home if orders are given to evacuate. If you can stay home, keep away from windows and doors. Stay in a hallway or first floor room without windows.

Have these items in your emergency storm kit.
Make sure there is enough for your family and pets
to last at least three days:

- canned, dried, or boxed food that won't spoil
- a can opener
- bottled water
- first-aid supplies
- flashlight with batteries
- battery-powered radio
- extra batteries for the flashlight and radio
- pet food
- a whistle to alert rescue workers to your location

Hurricanes can bring dangerous winds and surging
floods. Respect their awesome power and take smart steps
to stay safe.

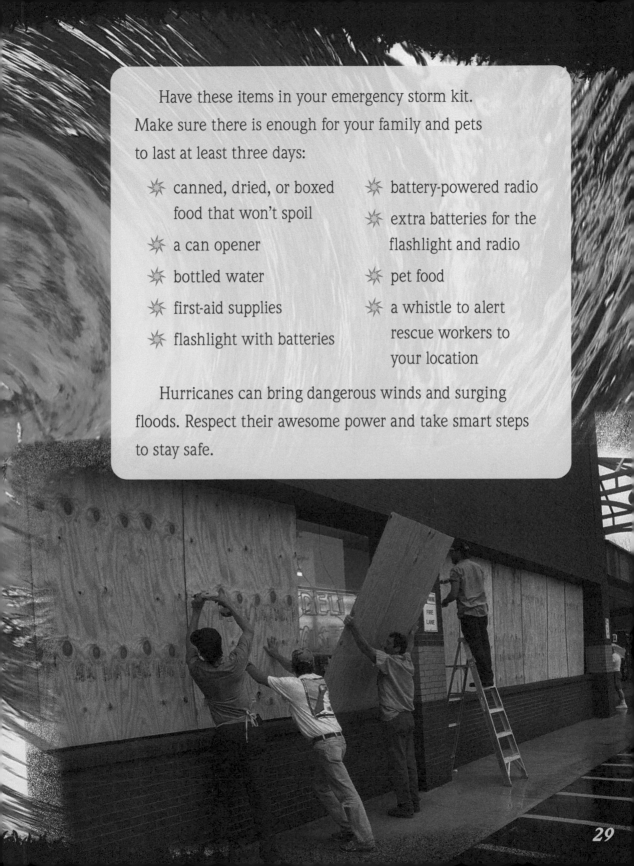

GLOSSARY

debris (duh-BREE)—the scattered pieces of something that has been broken or destroyed

evacuate (i-VA-kyuh-wayt)—to leave a dangerous place and go somewhere safer

eye (EYE)—the central, calm area at the center of a hurricane

famine (FA-muhn)—serious shortage of food resulting in widespread hunger and death

hurricane warning (HURH-ih-kane WOR-ning)—issued when a hurricane is expected to hit an area

hurricane watch (HURH-ih-kane WATCH)—issued when a hurricane may develop in an area

inland (IN-luhnd)—away from the ocean

landfall (LAND-fawl)—the area where a hurricane moves over land

levee (LEV-ee)—a structure or raised area built to hold back water and prevent flooding

marsh (MARSH)—an area of wet, low land

mudslide (MUHD-slide)—a flow of rock, earth, and debris mixed with water

radar (RAY-dar)—a weather tool that sends out waves to determine the size, strength, and movement of storms

stall (STAWL)—to come to a stop

storm surge (STORM SURJ)—a huge wave of water pushed ashore by an approaching hurricane

READ MORE

Carson, Mary Kay. *Inside Hurricanes.* Inside Series. New York: Sterling Publishing, 2010.

Royston, Angela. *Hurricanes! Eyewitness Disaster.* New York: Marshall Cavendish Benchmark, 2011.

Spilsbury, Louise. *Howling Hurricanes.* Awesome Forces of Nature. Chicago: Heinemann Library, 2010.

INTERNET SITES

FactHound offers a safe, fun way to find Internet sites related to this book. All of the sites on FactHound have been researched by our staff.

Here's all you do:

Visit *www.facthound.com*

Type in this code: 9781429676595

Super-cool stuff!

Check out projects, games and lots more at
www.capstonekids.com

INDEX